D1449658

100 REASONS TO LOVE
RYAN GOSLING

Joanna Benecke

Plexus, London

Introduction
Oh My Gosling!
The Gos-pel of Ryan

Welcome, fellow Gosfan. I'm glad to see you take your Ryligion seriously. Whatever your Ryan needs are, you've come to the right place. You will be understood here. You will be nurtured. Are you Blue because Ryan's not your Valentine? Maybe you're a Real Girl (or Guy) waiting for Ry-Ry to Drive you Crazy-Stupid in Love? Or maybe you're a Believer who knows that All Good Things come to those who keep a Notebook full of mildly psychotic I-AM-MRS-RYAN-GOSLING scribbles? (Don't worry, we all do it.)

There are many reasons to nurture an obsession with Mr Ryan Thomas Gosling (in addition to the obvious six that are packed so snugly in his stomach region): he acts, he sings, he carries his dog, he plays the ukulele, he breaks up street brawls, he's chivalrous-yet-feminist, he looks good in velvet, he loves strong women, he promotes peace, equality, love and cow horns – and then there's his intense-but-dopey-puppy-dog expression, which enables him to Fracture our minds and pin our hearts firmly in a Half Nelson. Phew. #PleaseExcuseMeWhileIGoDrool.

From his humble beginnings as the only Canuck Mouseketeer alongside fellow mice Britney, Xstina and Justin, via some rather frightening experiments with Nick-Carteresque middle partings, Ry-Go has progressed from playing freaks and geeks to the sort of top-billed heartthrob-with-a-cause roles that his idol Jimmy Dean would have fought him to the death for. Whether he's getting his sexy badboy on in *Drive* and *The Place Beyond the Pines*, or heart-breakingly falling apart in *Blue Valentine* and *All Good Things*, he's just so much hotter than all the other actors in Hollywood – and consequently all other men on this earth – put together. Sure, the Twihards would have us believe that no one does pale-and-interesting better than Robert Pattinson – but have they *seen* Ryan in *The United States of Leland*? *So* pale. *So* interesting. SO HOT. R-Patz looks like an anaemic, long-toothed baby shrimp in comparison.

From one Ryhard to another, let me tell it to you straight: Ryan is, quite simply, the shit. And yet he doesn't realise it himself! In his own words: "Well, I'm not that good-looking. I'm a pretty weird-looking guy." Although such statements raise concerns regarding his Rysight, they also score him some major modesty points – which makes him even *more* the shit. #ItsEnoughToGiveUsRyaneurysms.

These days it's pretty much only R-G himself who doesn't see his own hotness. Gone are the times when, as he puts it, "I would try to get commercials and my face wouldn't sell anything." Say *what*? Who *were* these deluded casting directors? The Gosface could sell us absolutely anything – even Mohawks for dogs. (Yup, Ry shaves his pooch for summer so the poor mutt doesn't overheat. So much aww.)

Clearly there are trillions of reasons to love the Gos, but I've carefully selected the 100

most important ones and gathered them together in this handy volume, complete with a whole lot of pictorial and pectoral evidence for you to examine. Closely. (BTW, the pages aren't saliva-proof, so go easy on the licking.)

Whether you've had Goslingitis for years or have only recently succumbed to this wondrous condition, I sincerely hope that *100 Reasons to Love Ryan Gosling* will prove invaluable in aiding your obsessive lifestyle. It can also be used as a manual by which to judge exactly how inferior all other men are to his Gosness. (And yes, there are pictures of Ryan's pecs.)

Here endeth the intro. Please commence with the Ry-eading.

1. Being a Mouseketeer didn't f**k him up

Unlike Britney, Xstina and Justin, Ry-Ry has yet to manifest any obvious mental scars from his childhood days at Disney. (Though, like Ms Spears, Ryan has been known to shave his head – but I reckon we can all agree he wore it best.) Even as a twelve-year-old he asserted that he didn't care about his friends calling him "Mouse Boy" as he knew it was affectionate. Aww. (This was before he got sick of being bullied, watched *Rambo*, thought he *was* Rambo and took steak knives to school . . .)

2. He taught Britney Spears about sex

Back when Brit was still a girl, not yet a (shaven-headed) woman, lickel Wyan filled his pre-teen colleague in on the facts of life. In fact, he shared his knowledge with all the Mouseketeers. "I just told them what I heard – like positions and stuff. All the other mothers went to Disney and told them I was corrupting their kids." (Guess Mama Spears didn't want her daughter driven Crazy by a tweeny Gosling.) RyRy feels particularly guilty about contributing to Britney becoming not-that-innocent. "I feel somewhat responsible for how sexual she is now [. . .] When I see her with a snake around her neck, I think: Did I do that?" I hate to break it to you, Ry, but you've made us *all* sexual. Face it, we're Slaves 4 U.

3. He's Herculean

His first acting job in LA was the title role in a TV series called *Young Hercules*. Ry played a teenaged version of the Roman god famous for undertaking twelve tasks of herculean magnitude (was that even *in* the Disney version?), including a lot of slaying and capturing – but also a spot of cleaning. Hello typecasting. I always knew Ryan wasn't just a god: he's a god with a task list. Hot *and* organized. Drool.

4. Backstreet Boycott

The Backstreet Boys asked Ry-Go to audition for the band, but he turned them down. This was a really great call. (Don't believe me? Google recent pics of A.J. and Howie for pictorial evidence of BSB facial wreckage. Man, their battery really *is* low.)

5. He plays jazz guitar

Jazz . . . That one little syllable that makes "guitar" sound so much deeper, moodier and more desirable.

6. He's Canadian

There's something politically friendly, culturally quirky, syrupy sweet – and just plain *sexy* aboot Canada, eh?

7. He's good with kids

Okay, so *Drive*Ryan's "Hey, you want a toothpick?" may not be the best kiddie chat we've ever heard, but it's followed by that disgustingly cute scene where Ry smiles goofy-gorgeously as he watches cartoons with Carey Mulligan's weirdly silent little boy. And then there's the adorability of Ryan's relationship with his obscenely cute daughter in *Blue Valentine*. When he lifts her up and cuddles her we're so torn – part of us want to *be* her, part of us wants the Gos to fertilize our eggs ASAP so that we can *make* her. Decisions, decisions . . . Anyway, I know those on-screen instances of Amazing-Father-Figureness were just acting, but the RyMan genuinely cares about da kidz, which is why his band Dead Man's Bones chose to record an album with the Silverlake Children's Choir. But it wasn't just LA sprogs who got to sing with the Bones; when they went on tour the band used a different local children's choir at every show. So not only is Ry-Gos super-musical – singing, songwriting and instrumenting all over the shop – he also wants to help a new generation score hipster points. Forget Jack Black, R-G is the Coolest. Music. Teacher. Ever. Bring on School of Ryock.

8. His drummer name is "Little Goose"

Not only does this show that he's up on semantics, but it's also high-level-fluffy cute. Added bonus points to his Gosness for not actually *being* a mere drummer (we all know they're the shelf-stackers of rock). He and Dead Man's Bones bandmate Zach Shields share the singing, songwriting and music-playing in a gorgeous utopian vision of fairness, equality and chilled coolness. (Not dissimilar to Canada.)

9. *The Notebook*

I feel it's unnecessary to go into more detail. Just look at the picture of Ryan and hear him say the following words. To you. With his gorgeous (slightly weird) voice from his gorgeous lips in his gorgeous face. "So it's not gonna be easy. It's going to be really hard. We're gonna have to work at this every day, but I want to do that because I want you. I want all of you, forever, every day. You and me . . . every day." Now please excuse me while I go fall into a lust coma.

10. Public displays of torso

The Gosling is not afraid to get naked on screen. Thank God. We've seen his perfect torso everywhere, from its early exposure in *The Notebook*, via the swimming scene in *All Good Things*, to the prolonged romping absfest that is *Crazy, Stupid, Love*. And what makes Gos different from other flesh-happy actors is the fact that he chooses movies that would be good movies even without the nakedness! Which leads me to my next point.

11. He makes boyfriend-proof movies too

Sure, they may have objections to *The Notebook* (allegations of its innate chick-flickery can be hard to negate, what with the rowing and the lake and the swans and the schmaltz and the I-love-you-sooo-much-even-though-you've-got-Alzheimer's), but no man can object to being made to watch and rewatch *Drive*. For the fast cars and high-calibre performances, of course. Although it may be tempting to stop the film after Ryan's long and sultry kiss with that #luckybitch Carey Mulligan, thereby ending the movie on a high before heads and faces get smashed in, boyfriends will probably call this cheating.

12. Interest in international cuisine

In the mood for Moroccan? No sweat, Ryan runs the restaurant Tagine in Beverly Hills. Now that's moorish.

13. Jazz guitar

I know, I already mentioned this. But seriously. *Jazz. Guitar.*

14. He invented "geeky killer cute"

In 2003's *The United States of Leland*, Ryface plays a shaggy-haired, weird (but hot) kid accused of a gruesome killing. So far, so Kevin. But here's the thing – although it all gets a bit pretentious and plastic-bag-floating-around-representing-life-man, it's still loads less po-faced than the mournfest that is *We Need to Talk About Kevin*. And boy do we envy that #luckybitch Jena Malone when Ry leans in to hug her and tell her that everything will be all right. (So what if he viciously stabbed her special needs brother?) Plus, there are loads of slow shots of the Gosface in the sun, making it excellent background viewing. Sort of like a moving poster. Oh, and this film shows that Ryan looks good as a brunette. Not only is his acting versatile, but so is his hair.

15. He's romantic (in a weird way)

"If I eat a huge meal and I can get the girl to rub my belly, I think that's about as romantic as I can think of."

And bromantic

His old roommate is none other than fellow ex-Mouseketeer Justin Timberlake. The pair lived together while filming *The Mickey Mouse Club* because the RyMom had to return to Canada for work, leaving her RyChild in the custody of Mama Timberlake. According to JT, the pair used to swagger around speaking in faux-gangsta style. "We thought we were so cool when we were on *The Mickey Mouse Club*." Who would have thought that the cutest mousemates ever would grow up to bring so much sexy back into our lives?

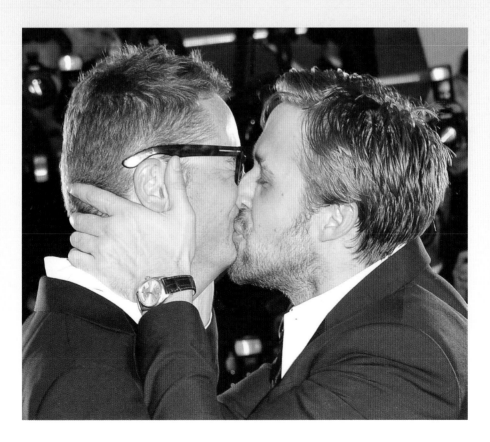

16. JT clearly misses being Ryan's mousemate

Justin reminisces with misty mouse eyes. "Aw, man, we were crazy. We like, skipped tutoring. Going to the park, to the *Honey I Shrunk the Kids* set. We'd have milkshakes. Oh, man, we were so gangsta." We get it, Timbo; living with Ryan would be the highlight of anyone's life.

17. He's a real carpenter

Well, sort of. R-Gos made the kitchen table featured in *The Notebook* in preparation for playing the role of Noah. So he's definitely handy. And method-acty. (But not in a Daniel Day-Lewis, I'm-gonna-beat-you-to-death-whilst-dancing-in-a-bowling-alley-'cos-that's-what-my-character'd-do kind of way.)

18. He takes his mother with him to premieres

(But not in the way Kevin Spacey used to . . .)

19. He took his girlfriend with him to his mom's graduation

In summer 2012, RyGo took Eva Mendes – that #luckybitch every Gosfan would switch places with in a heartbeat – on holiday to Canada to watch his mother Donna graduate from Ontario's Brock University with a teaching degree. In an attempt to keep a low profile, the Gos refused to pose for photos with fans. An official at the college said, "He didn't want his celebrity status to distract from his mom's big day and all of the other grads' big day." Yeah, right. As if any of those lucky Canucky students will remember anything aboot that day, save for the wondrous fact that Ryan Gosling went to their graduation. (Oh, and incidentally, Mrs Gosling, now you're qualified, please teach us how to have sons that look like Ryan.)

20. His social conscience

Showing his support for animals and kids, Ry's a keen supporter of charities including PETA, Invisible Children and the Enough Project. He's travelled to Chad, Uganda and the Congo to raise awareness about conflicts in the regions. All this and he still finds time to be my screensaver.

21. He has good taste in movies (most of the time)

Thankfully Ryan had the sense to drop out of ickfest *The Lovely Bones* before filming started. He was replaced by Mark Wahlberg, who jumped at the chance to don a dodgy beige polo neck and play the super-fun role of a dead girl's grieving dad. If only R-G had displayed the same nous when it came to the damp squib that is *Gangster Squad*. We wouldn't have had to snore through it if Marky Mark was the star. We would've just stayed home and re-re-re-watched the first half of *Drive*.

22. He makes politics
hot on-screen

In political drama *The Ides of March*, he somehow manages to make George Clooney look like an airbrushed alligator compared to the beauty of his royal Ryness.

23. He makes
politics
hot off-
screen

By marching his gorgeous body alongside the Occupy Wall Street

protestors. It's official: the 99% love Ryan (and so do the other 1%).

24. He makes politics hot in screen-meets-life

Ryan produced and narrated *ReGeneration*, a documentary about the political apathy of the young, the Occupy Wall Street movement, and the bankers and corporations who have caused so much socio-economic woe. Right on. Ry-on.

25. He chose his own accent

Already exhibiting that famous I-don't-follow-the-crowd-'cos-I-think-deeply-about-stuff attitude as a child, lickel Wyan decided to carve out a new accent for himself. He felt the Canadian lilt wasn't tough enough, so modelled his speech on Marlon Brando. So now you know why he sounds so damn sexyweird; it's Gawdfatha via aboot.

26. He's happy to be pulped for the good of the movie

RyRy's not one of those egomaniacs who only wants to play superheroes. (Did someone just cough-mention Governor Schwarzenegger?) While in *Drive* Ry's the one doing the pummelling, on the set of gritty bloodfest *Only God Forgives* he suggested major changes to the screenplay because he felt it would be totally ridic for his character to single-handedly beat up a highly-skilled Muay Thai martial arts expert. The changes were made and, as R-Gos himself puts it, "I don't think I land one punch on anyone, it's just having my ass handed to me the whole time . . . and it's more realistic."

27. He loves animals

Ry has described his dog, George, as his "soulmate". (Eva Mendes was unavailable for comment.) George Gosling, to give him his full name, gets to go to places that ordinary canines rarely do – i.e. on talk shows and into Ryan's arms whenever Ryan carries him – not walks him, *carries* him – through airports. Ryan and George's bond is one of perfect love and trust, apparently designed to melt the average woman's heart into a warm puddle of pheromones and corn syrup. I, for one, would happily be Ryan's bitch. But I know he's far too feminist to ever use a word like that.

28. He doesn't buy into The Game

While prepping for the role of pickup artist extraordinaire Jacob in *Crazy, Stupid, Love*, Ry did a lot of research into chatting up girls (he suffers for his art), including reading up on popular girl-snaring technique *The Game*. Basically, the rules of said Game are to unnerve and unsettle the victim (I mean girl) by saying negative things about her and coming across as a confident a-hole who doesn't really like her and thinks he could do better. The idea is that she will then be so confused and keen to please that she'll do anything to hook up with you. Great! Deception, calculation and humiliation: sounds like the perfect start to a happy relationship (if your life is scripted by E.L. James). Obviously his Ryness was not a fan of this icky method. "I read that book, *The Game*. I like to call it The Lame."

29. He can do the *Dirty Dancing* body lift

As he so ably (and abs-ly) demonstrated with that #luckybitch Emma Stone in *C, S, L*. That's *the* body lift. That Patrick Swayze and Jennifer Grey did. While "(I've Had) The Time of My Life" played. In *Dirty Dancing*. The film that defines every girl's youth. Even if Ryan was unable to do anything else except breathe and chew, this ability alone would still make him prime marriage material.

30. His taste in women

Sure, Mr Gosling likes his women über-beautiful, but he also wants them to be intelligent and independent. Names in his little black book include not only Sandra Bullock and Rachel McAdams, but also Blake Lively and Olivia Wilde. And we completely fit right in with that awesome lady crew. Totally. Don't hate them at all.

31. His ex-girlfriends love him

Even when they're no longer "in" love with him (though they blatantly still are, let's face facts). Just ask Bullock and McAdams – not a bad word to say about RyRy between them. Not even a mild gripe about how he always leaves the toilet seat up, farts in bed or spends too much time gelling his hair and oiling his pecs. This is clearly further proof of Ryan's genetically-measurable superiority to the rest of the male race. It's no surprise that the first thing Rach McAds did after her recent split with boyf Michael Sheen was to speed dial the Gos. Going from Ryan's s-pec-tacular physique to Mike's squirrel face was a serious downgrade. No wonder E-Mend is worried R-Mc will try and reclaim R-Gos! Who could blame her?

32. He can look good in anything

Yes, anything:

33. Nerd glasses and a wifebeater

When looking intellectual-but-hard in *The Ides of March*.

34. White satin jacket – *quilted* – with a scorpion embroidered on the back, teamed with freaky leather Catwoman gloves

It might come from RuPaul's

wardrobe, but boy does it look

hot on *Drive*Ryan.

35. Gone-to-seed and balding with dirty cargo pants, sweatshirt – with an *eagle's head* on it – tinted glasses and out-of-control facial hair at the beginning (which-is-the-end) of *Blue Valentine*

He should look like Paul Giamatti playing a 1970s serial killer. Instead he looks cute.

36. Double denim

In *All Good Things* he commits the ultimate fashion crime (before committing some pretty nasty murders). But in the Gos's case crime does pay. No one's looked so good in head-to-toe jeans, not even James Dean. Oh and Ry's a bit ginger in this film. But he still manages to look smokin' hot! What the freckles is that about?

37. He is the only person who can wear a velvet suit

And look good in it. Russell Brand must be f**king furious.

38. He's 6'2"

Tall, but not crazy b-ball tall.

39. He has tiny cute little ears
Each one is a miniature work of art.

40. He's never worn his underwear on top of his pants

Speculation is rife as to which superhero movie RyRy will lose his comic-book virginity to. When an interviewer suggested to him that he could play The Flash in upcoming movie *Justice League* (which, *Avengers Assemble*-style, brings together a host of the usual Bat and Supermen, who don't understand the meaning of "under" wear), he didn't seem desperate to audition. "Here's the thing. *Drive* was my attempt at the superhero movie. I had a costume and everything. The scorpion jacket. It was like my cape." Okay, Ry, we've embraced the drag-queen jacket. Fact is, we know that Ryan doesn't need to play a superhero because he *is* one.

41. He breaks up street brawls

And he does it wearing a sexy stripy vest top. If you google "Ryan Gosling breaking up fight", you can see amateur phone footage of RyRy in action. No need to trust the tweenage girls' shouts of, "Aaaahhhh, it's that guy from *The Notebook*." You'll know for sure it's him as soon as you lay eyes on those perfect, peace-loving arms. No matter that Ryan later admitted he shouldn't have stepped in because the guy he was protecting turned out to be stealing from a street vendor. A case of Ryan indulging in some aiding and abs-betting . . . Oh well. I'm still gonna swoon.

42. He saves British people's lives

No, not just by being so much more perfect, toned and cool than any British person could ever hope to be – he literally actually saved the life of a British journalist who was about to be knocked down by a car in New York before Ry whisked her to safety. Oh, to be that confused British lady who forgot about right-hand drive and was rewarded with a hug from Ryan. (But however much you want a Goshug, the stepping-out-into-a-busy-road method has only been known to work once and could seriously damage your health. Use at your own peril.)

43. He's not a Culkin

While lickel Wyan and Macaulay Culkin shared many similarities back when they were kids – both blond, disgustingly-cute child stars born in 1980 – it's fair to say that poor old Mac definitely got the shittier deal. Sure, initially the odds were stacked in his favour: while Wyan was being underused on *The Mickey Mouse Club* ("It was kind of depressing because when I got there, they realised that I wasn't really up to snuff in comparison with what some of the other kids were able to do . . . occasionally I'd have a sketch here or there, but I didn't end up working that much, which was disheartening"), Mac was the highest-paid child star in history. But then the tables turned. While Ryan became ever hotter and more castable, Maccy C descended into a freaky-eyed, grungy pit of drugs and obscurity, divorcing his parents and getting married – and separated – before he turned twenty. (Remember those pics of him with long blue hair? Mega shudder.) It has been observed that if Ryan and Steve Buscemi had a baby it would be Macaulay Culkin. Check the internet for photos – people have put a lot of work into this theory.

44. He'd have been amazing in *Home Alone*

With his innate social conscience, there's no way Ryan would have tortured those deluded burglars with such inhumane glee. He'd either have stared at them with his kind, intelligent-but-dopey eyes and discussed their life choices through the medium of ukulele – or he'd have just slit their throats, swiftly and cleanly. None of that booby trap bullshit. Bring on *Drive Home Alone.*

45. He's not a Mormon

He somehow managed to grow up not-a-Mormon in a Mormon household. In his own words: "I wasn't really Mormon, my parents were. My mom was really cool. She said, 'This is an option, but this isn't the only option. This is an idea, but this isn't the only idea. You have to find your own truth.'" When asked about Mormonism, Gos has said, "I never really could identify with it." That's lucky, because one thing Mormons ain't allowed to do is watch R-rated movies. And I'm guessing the rule also prohibits Mormons from appearing in them? So a Mormon Ryan wouldn't have given us *Drive* or *Blue Valentine*. But luckily this isn't so, and his torso is forever captured on celluloid in all its pectoral beauty.

46. But he could *play* a Mormon?

Dare we hope that maybe maybe maaaybe the Ryling would consider putting his singing, dancing, comedy and ex-Mormon skills to good use by appearing in a future movie version of *The Book of Mormon*? (And please can he be naked in it?)

47. He has his priorities straight

"Sometimes I think that the one thing I love most about being an adult is the right to buy candy whenever and wherever I want." Okay. For me it's all about the fact that I can watch Ryan's R- and NC-17-rated movies, but, hey, each to their own.

48. He's found his funny

"I don't like to be entertaining. I don't like the feeling of being entertaining. If there was a musical or a comedy that was not just for entertainment but was rooted in something I could relate to on a real level, then I think I would do it." Thank God Ryan could relate to Jacob, the egocentric womaniser with a penchant for nudity, or we'd have no *Crazy, Stupid, Love* . . .

49. He believes in marriage equality

And he has the t-shirt to prove it. But hands off guys, just because he approves of dudes marrying dudes doesn't mean he isn't going to marry a girl (aka me).

50. His agent loves him

And not just now he's a superstar. Apparently his agent "believed" in him so strongly that she offered to give him money so he could focus on his "craft" and not have to take non-acting jobs. Really? An agent did that for the love of the "craft"? Or was it the love of the pecs? (Ry is quick to point out that he didn't take her up on the offer.)

51. He really really likes women

"I like working with actresses, and I like women a lot, not for obvious reasons, but just in that there's so much about what they bring to the scene that keeps it so interesting. Their instincts are so different, and they never explain them to you." It's not surprising that the RyMan loves the ladies, not just because the feeling is so deeply mutual, but because he grew up surrounded by women. His dad was away from home a lot, working as a travelling salesman for a paper mill, and then refused to move with the family to the USA to pursue RyRy's career. So they moved without Papa Gosling and Ryan became the man of the family. "I don't think anyone can teach you how to be a man but a woman. You only learn by learning what they need." Does he read our minds before he makes these statements?

52. He doesn't live up his own ass

While he's been know to get pretty bogged down in prepping for roles – e.g. living in a bedsit, refusing to talk to friends and calling himself "Danny" in preparation for making *The Believer*, or learning to be a badass motorcyclist and taking advice from former bank robbers for *The Place Beyond the Pines* – he always remains fairly grounded. "Acting isn't that hard, really. I mean, I think that people make a big deal about it, but you just kind of try to say your lines naturally. You try to make them sound like you're saying them for the first time, but that's about it." Totally. It's not exactly brain rocket science surgey, is it?

53. He really truly honestly never expected to be a sex symbol

"The director [of *The Notebook*], Nick Cassavetes, called me to meet him at his house. When I got there, he was standing in his back yard, and he looked at me and said, 'I want you to play this role because you're not like the other young actors out there in Hollywood. You're not handsome, you're not cool, you're just a regular guy who looks a bit nuts.'" That's so weird, because last time I checked the dictionary entries for both "cool" and "handsome" there was just a picture of Ryan's face.

54. He left his mark at school

Despite spending a lot of his childhood out of school filming or being home-schooled – and dropping out of high school at seventeen to go off and be Hercules – it's unlikely that any teacher or pupil will ever forget him. And not just because he was a Disney kid who went on to become a movie star. "[I] wanted to be Arnold Schwarzenegger, and I really wanted to be Sylvester Stallone. When I first saw *Rambo*, that movie put a kind of spell on me and I actually thought I *was* Rambo. So much so that, one day, I took a bunch of steak knives to school and threw them around at recess time because I thought we were in the movie! I'm not proud of this but I did learn a lesson – I was suspended from school and my mother said I couldn't watch R-rated movies anymore." Not to self: chucking steak knives around is a really good way to make sure people remember you.

55. He was home-schooled

I know, I know, normally the mention of home and schooling in the same sentence would scare the shit out of me (have you seen the movie *Jesus Camp*?), but in this case it's just cool. Ten-year-old Wyan spent a year at home with his mother watching movies and listening to Chet Baker and Billie Holiday. He says it gave him "a sense of autonomy that I've never really lost". I say it gave him a sense of hey-girl-wanna-hear-me-play-jazz-guitar cool.

56. He'll do cheesy weird shit

Like appearing in Funny or Die's *Drunk History Christmas* sketch, alongside that #luckybitch E-Mend and Jim Carrey, where he mimes to a drunk man reciting "Twas the Night Before Christmas". If you've ever wondered what Ry and Eva look like in bed together – wearing nightgowns and nightcaps – this one's for you.

57. He knows he's a bit of a weirdo

"When I was a kid, I was walking to school and I saw a guy on a motorcycle get hit. I walked up to where he was lying on the road, he looked up at me, and my first thought was, 'I got to get a motorcycle!' What can I say? Clearly there's something wrong with my brain!"

58. He's a dog-whisperer

Gos has revealed the following about his dog's innermost thoughts: "He looks like a little guy in a suit, and he doesn't like it that he's a dog, you can tell." Erm, you can? Whatever you say, Ryanimal.

59. He's more likely to get a random doodle than a girlfriend's name tattooed on his arm

"A tattoo should never be meaningful, because at a certain point you're going to hate it, and it might as well make you laugh." (Though, to be fair, the name "Sandra Bullock" is pretty hilarious.) Also, for those of you who can't sleep at night for fear you'll wake up to the news that Ry's *Place Beyond the Pines* face tat won't scrub off, you can rest easy. He was never a fan of the tattooed teardrop: "I said to [the director] Derek, 'I got to lose this face tattoo. It's the worst. It's so distracting and it's going to ruin everything.' And he said, 'Well, I'm sure that's how people with face tattoos feel. So now you have to pay the consequences of your actions.' So I had to do the whole film with it and now see it on posters. It gave me a sense of shame that I feel was inherent to the character." Oh and speaking of Ryan and tats, do you remember Ryan Cabrera? No, nor do I, but he was apparently some never-popular singer back in the 2000s – though he was more famous for dating Ashlee Simpson – and he's recently had Ryan Gosling's FACE tattooed on his LEG. Yes, that's the Gosface smeared over some hasn't-been's shin. Thinking about it, it's probably the best thing Ryan Cabrera's ever done.

60. He managed to make us want to marry a crack-addicted inner-city schoolteacher

How he does this is the main mystery of *Half Nelson*.

61. He's the only guy who can make having a relationship with a life-size doll uncreepy

And he does it while sporting a weird-ass moustache. And his name is Lars . . .

62. He's impossible to forget

Let's face it, although he didn't get much screen time, all we actually remember from *Remember the Titans* is Ryan. Apparently the movie's a super-serious dissection of racial tension in sport. But all I recall is RyRy's cute'n'camp dancing in the locker room.

63. He's a Scorpio

Not that I really believe in star signs, but "Scorpio" is a pretty sexy word. (Unlike, say, "Cancer".)

64. With his hair dyed platinum for *The Place Beyond the Pines*, you can clearly see that the *Harry Potter* character he'd play would be Draco Malfoy

And I think we'd all love to see his magic wand.

65. He's always had Drive

When he was a teenager (shortly after that whole I-am-Rambo-with-steak-knives incident), Ryan was put in a special-needs class, diagnosed with ADHD and prescribed Ritalin for a while. However, he wasn't keen on the drug and realised that he didn't need to medicate for hyper-activity – it was just his ambition and drive fizzing away inside him, because he wanted to do amazing things like make movies and albums and play the ukulele.

(Or could it have been the after-effects of two years at Disney? Look what it did to Li-Lo . . .)

66. Aged eleven, Wyan appeared on stage in black shiny Hammer pants and a three-tone shirt, singing "When a Man Loves a Woman"

YouTube it. Now.

67. When he's finished singing, eleven-year-old Wyan then proceeds to dance with his sister Mandi to the C&C Music Factory track "Gonna Make You Sweat (Everybody Dance Now)"

Watch it again. I know part of you is kind of fantasising about being Wyan's stage mom. Yes, that's a bit creepy, but we all do it, so it's okay.

68. His favourite movie is
East of Eden

Excellent. I'm totally happy to watch James Dean (wearing double denim) with Ryan (wearing anything or nothing), whenever. To be honest, I'll watch any movie Ryan wants. Especially if Ryan's in it.

69. While at school, his nickname was "Trouble"

Probably because he was always sticking up for the girls and quoting feminist philosophers, right? Or maybe it was those steak knives . . .

70. Even before he grew those perfect muscles he knew he wanted to entertain us

"I always wanted to entertain. When I was six, a scrawny, scrawny kid, I'd get in my red speedos and do muscle moves. I actually thought I was muscular. I didn't know everyone was laughing at me." Aw, it's like *Crazy, Stupid, Love: The Preschool Years*. But growing the muscles was a great move, Wyan. A sleek, bulbous, beautiful move.

71. He has great taste in t-shirts

In addition to his pro-gay marriage shirt, Ry-Gos has been papped wearing both a "Darfur" and a "Macaulay Culkin" t-shirt, proving that he's keen to show his support for the vulnerable.

72. He likes knitting

"I did this scene in *Lars and the Real Girl* where I was in a room full of old ladies who were knitting, and it was an all-day scene, so they showed me how. It was one of the most relaxing days of my life. If I had to design my perfect day, that would be it. And you get something out of it at the end. You get a nice present. For someone who wants an oddly shaped, off-putting scarf."

73. He loves granddad sweaters

His fav is a reddish-brown knitted affair with grey, white and black tessellated shapes at the top. Buy it for your boyfriend — who'll probably look weird in it — and call him Ryan.

74. He stopped Peter O'Toole leching over his sister

At the Oscars in 2007, acting veteran Peter O'Fool was getting a little bit too forward with Mandi Gosling. Ryan explained, "He did it for what I felt was too long, and I had to step in. I said, 'Hey Peter, you're a legend and all, but you're going to have to get your hands off my sister.'" Mandi, we'd be so jealous of you if incest wasn't illegal.

75. He says he isn't funny but he clearly is

Just ask Carey Mulligan — he made her roar with laughter on the set of *Drive* and she was heartbroken at the time. (Though obviously anyone would get over a failed romance with Shia LaBeouf if they spent five minutes with Ryan.) Carey says that Ryan "makes you laugh all day". Aww. #LuckyBitch.

76. He still can't believe people think he's hot

"I'm not that good-looking. I think I'm a pretty weird-looking guy. Every role I got up until *The Notebook* was the weirdo, freak, psychopath, nerd, outsider character guy." Seriously Gos, your lack of self-esteem is getting Rydiculous.

77. Raquel Welch (and a Muppet spider)
inspired him to act

"I was a lonely child, I didn't do well at school and TV was my only friend. Then, one day, I saw Raquel Welch on *The Muppet Show*. She was dancing with this big furry spider and I immediately fell in love. She was the first crush I ever had, and I thought, 'How do I get to meet this woman?' And then I thought, 'Well, she's on TV, so to meet her I have to get on TV myself.'"

78. He has been known to blow into conch shells

While taking a break from shooting the latest Terrence Malick art installation – I mean movie – in Merida, Mexico, the Gosbreath was papped taking a solitary moment to blow into a large conch shell. Whether he was making sweet music – 'cos ukuleles are *so* last season – or recreating a scene from Lord of the Rys, I don't know. Safe to say I know about five million women who would eat their own spleens to *be* that shell.

79. He makes deaf kids happy

Ryan turned up at a fundraiser at Texas School for the Deaf in Austin. Not only did he pose for photos with the kids and parents – and pay $50 for one dollar's worth of glow-in-the-dark cotton candy – but he also insisted on being taught to sign "please" and "thank you" so he could thank the children individually. What's the sign for "swoon f**king overload"?

80. He knows how to show a girl a good time

For a first class Rydate he'll take you to either a) Disneyland for cotton candy and public displays of affection, or b) a Parisian graveyard to mourn at Jim Morrison's tomb. (He's taken E-Mend to both. I think we can all agree that she's just rubbing our faces in it at this point.)

81. He wants to date us

Well, sort of. I mean, he's basically said as much. Because, despite a string of famous #luckybitch girlfriends, the Ryboy is sceptical about high-profile relationships. "Show-business is the bad guy. When both people are in show-business it's too much show-business. It takes all of the light, so nothing else can grow." Watch out E-Mend, there's a swarm of non-famous girl-next-doors just waiting to grow on Ry!

82. He gives his dog a Mohawk for the summer

George needs to keep cool. I can totally sympathise. It must be hard not to get

hot and bothered when you're being carried around in Ryan's herculean arms.

83. Even super-cool actresses get star-struck when kissing Ryan

Evan Rachel Wood on her sex scene in *Rydes of March*: "Yeah, it was awesome. We had fun. Ryan's amazing because he has this way about him that's incredibly attractive, not just in a sexy way but he's smart, he's cool. He has this mysterious quality to him that drives people crazy, so yeah, it wasn't a hard day at work." I *bet* you had fun. Smug much?

84. "Don't call her baby!"

Ry-Ry yelled this at a photographer who had the audacity to address Eva Mendes in such an over-familiar way. (I am totally, absolutely convinced that Gos's objection was based on feminist principles rather than macho jealousy.)

85. His response to Gosline

British streaming service Blinkbox set up a helpline called the Gosline to aid distraught Gosfans struggling to deal with Ryan's announcement that he's going to take a break from acting. For a "standard fee" the depressed and desperate can call up and listen to famous lines from Gosmovies like *The Notebook*, because, let's face it, *It's not gonna be easy. It's gonna be really hard; we're gonna have to work at this every day, but we want to do that because he wants us. He wants all of us, forever, every day. Him and us . . . every day. (Even if we get Alzheimer's.)* RyRy's reaction to hearing of this new helpline was: "I'm feeling a little freaked out, yeah. I'm feeling feelings of freaked-out-ness, sure." Of course you are, Ry, but there's an easy solution. Don't quit making movies. As long as you keep acting, we promise not to call the Gosline. Again.

86. He can see the lighter side of death

"I think about death a lot, like I think we all do. I don't think of suicide as an option, but as fun. It's an interesting idea that you can control how you go. It's this thing that's looming, and you can control it." Okay, that's a bit weird, but sure, cool, whatever – just as long as you know you can never ever die, Ry. Or we'll kill you.

87. When he was little he wanted to be a car

His childhood quirkiness included some serious auto-obsession. But not in your average wow-I-love-fast-cars-check-out-my-collection-of-Hot-Wheels way. Oh no, not R-Gos. Aged five, he managed to back the family car into the path of another vehicle, narrowly escaping a nasty accident. Then he developed a new hobby. "[I] stood in the middle of the street trying to get hit by cars, not because I wanted to die but I wanted to be where the cars were." In case you're worried that Ry grew up to be a car-spotting bore – don't be. "I can't drive like my character in the film [*Drive*] does. I didn't know anything about cars till I did that movie. Obviously, in order to play the part, I had to grow some kind of appreciation, so I bought a car for $200 from a lot that was like a graveyard for dead cars. The car was a 1973 Chevy Malibu, which we actually used as my car in the film." (No word on whether he still likes standing in the middle of moving traffic . . .)

88. Awards Schawards

Ryan missed the 2012 Golden Globes ceremony (despite a double nomination) because he was working "out of the country". That's the kind of stick-it-to-the-man, nobody-puts-me-in-no-box attitude we expect from Ry-Ry. Making your own rules is the height of hotness. (Though it might also explain why he hasn't won a Golden Globe yet.)

89. He loves Disney and has a childlike quality

(But not in the way Michael Jackson did.) This probably stems from over-exposure to Mickey Mouse at an impressionable age: "I went through puberty in a theme park. I'm grateful. That place was a landscape to me. I had adventures every day. Backstage at Disney World, there are stories. Mickey Mouse with his head off, drinking coffee on break. Pirates on the phone. Ghosts in line for food. It just made me see things." Hmm, this makes me less inclined to sell my firstborn to Disney when Ryan and I have kids.

90. He can play the ukulele

Without being annoying. Has anyone else *ever* achieved this?

91. Guys love him too

There are plenty of Ryguys out there. *Hunger Games* star Josh Hutcherson, for instance, really looks up to the Gosman. "I'm a big fan. I like his subtleties and how he really internalizes a lot of the emotion. And for me, that's kind of my style. So, he's definitely a big person to look up to." Aw, Ry is big, isn't he? Especially his beautiful, sculpted, bulging, snugglyarms.

92. He helps delivery men lug heavy boxes

When he saw the men struggling to empty a lorry full of stuff he'd ordered for his new house, Ryan came straight outside and assisted them. With his beautiful muscles. No word on whether he then helped them unpack an old war-veteran's room in a nursing home, showing great care and sensitivity, before bumping into Michelle Williams and giving her his number – but he probably did.

93. He spent New Year's Day 2012 with his two favourite women

Eva Mendes and his mom. The three of them saw a movie together. Let's hope it wasn't the godawful *New Year's Eve* . . .

94. He wants to be a dad

"I'd like to be making babies but I'm not, so I'm making movies. When someone comes along, I don't think I'll be able to do both and I'm fine with that. I'll make movies until I make babies. I have no idea when the handover will happen." You can't tease us like that, Ry, unless you plan to follow through. We're ready to have your babies whenever you are. Actually, scrap that, we're ready NOW.

95. He still doesn't believe his own hype

"Look, this is crazy. I don't understand how I'm here, living this life, wearing this suit. I assume I'm going to pay for it someday . . . And that's okay. It seems fair to me. I just want to be ready for it. I want to meet it like a gentleman." Don't sweat it, Ry, just take the suit off and come meet ME like a gentleman.

96. He can DJ

Dressed like Danny Zuko in white t-shirt, black pants and a motorcycle jacket, R-G's been known to spin his favourite tunes from the '40s and '50s at the Green Door Lounge's jazz night in Hollywood. Back in 2011, he also took charge of the decks at *Blue Valentine* producer Jamie Patricof's birthday party at the Roosevelt Hotel in LA. Jessica Alba and Nicole Richie were there – did my invite get lost in the mail or something?

97. He even makes cows horny

Ryanimal highlights atrocities we've never heard of before, such as the practice of de-horning dairy cows (udderly horrific). He wrote the following to the National Milk Producers Federation on behalf of PETA: "Dehorning is one of the most painful things done to cows on dairy farms, whether it is by burning a calf with a searing hot iron or applying caustic paste to create a chemical burn that eats away at the animal's flesh. There is absolutely no reason – and no excuse – for the cruel, unnecessary practice of dehorning to continue." Go Ry! Let's keep our cattle horny!